ARIA DA CAPO

BY EDNA ST. VINCENT MILLAY

——

THE HARP-WEAVER AND OTHER POEMS
SECOND APRIL
RENASCENCE AND OTHER POEMS
A FEW FIGS FROM THISTLES
ARIA DA CAPO: A PLAY
THE LAMP AND THE BELL: A DRAMA

ARIA DA CAPO

A PLAY IN ONE ACT

BY

EDNA ST. VINCENT MILLAY

Publishers

HARPER & BROTHERS

NEW YORK AND LONDON

ARIA DA CAPO

B-Y

ARIA DA CAPO

PERSONS

ARIA DA CAPO

A PLAY IN ONE ACT

SCENE
A Stage

*T*HE curtain rises on a stage set for a Harlequin-
ade, a merry black and white interior. Directly
behind the footlights, and running parallel with them,
is a long table, covered with a gay black and white
cloth, on which is spread a banquet. At the opposite
ends of this table, seated on delicate thin-legged chairs
with high backs, are Pierrot and Columbine, dressed
according to the tradition, excepting that Pierrot is
in lilac, and Columbine in pink. They are dining.

COLUMBINE: Pierrot, a macaroon! I cannot *live*
without a macaroon!

PIERROT: My only love,
You are *so* intense! . . . Is it Tuesday, Colum-
bine? —
I'll kiss you if it's Tuesday.

I

COLUMBINE: It is Wednesday,
If you must know. . . . Is this my artichoke,
Or yours?

PIERROT: Ah, Columbine,— as if it mattered!
Wednesday. . . . Will it be Tuesday, then,
    to-morrow,
By any chance?

COLUMBINE: To-morrow will be — Pierrot,
That isn't funny!

PIERROT: I thought it rather nice.
Well, let us drink some wine and lose our heads
And love each other.

COLUMBINE: Pierrot, don't you love
Me now?

PIERROT: La, what a woman! — how should I know?
Pour me some wine: I'll tell you presently.

COLUMBINE: Pierrot, do you know, I think you
    drink too much.

PIERROT: Yes, I dare say I do. . . . Or else
    too little.
It's hard to tell. You see, I am always wanting

A little more than what I have,—or else
A little less. There's something wrong. My dear,
How many fingers have you?

COLUMBINE: La, indeed,
How should I know?—It always takes me one
    hand
To count the other with. It's too confusing.
    Why?

PIERROT: Why?—I am a student, Columbine;
And search into all matters.

COLUMBINE: La, indeed?—
Count them yourself, then!

PIERROT: No. Or, rather, *nay*.
'Tis of no consequence. . . . I am become
A painter, suddenly,— and you impress me —
Ah, yes!—six orange bull's-eyes, four green pin-
    wheels,
And one magenta jelly-roll,— the title
As follows: *Woman Taking in Cheese from Fire-
    Escape.*

COLUMBINE: Well, I like that! So that is all I've
    meant
To you!

PIERROT: Hush! All at once I am become
A pianist. I will image you in sound. . . .
On a new scale. . . . Without tonality. . . .
Vivace senza tempo senza tutto. . . .
Title: *Uptown Express at Six O'Clock.*
Pour me a drink.

COLUMBINE: Pierrot, you work too hard.
You need a rest. Come on out into the garden,
And sing me something sad.

PIERROT: Don't stand so near me!
I am become a socialist. I love
Humanity; but I hate people. Columbine,
Put on your mittens, child; your hands are cold.

COLUMBINE: My hands are *not* cold!

PIERROT: Oh, I am sure they are.
And you must have a shawl to wrap about you,
And sit by the fire.

COLUMBINE: Why, I'll do no such thing!
I'm hot as a spoon in a teacup!

PIERROT: Columbine,
I'm a philanthropist. I know I am,
Because I feel so restless. Do not scream,
Or it will be the worse for you!

COLUMBINE: Pierrot,
My vinaigrette! I cannot *live* without
My vinaigrette!

PIERROT: My only love, you are
So fundamental! . . . How would you like to
be
An actress, Columbine? — I am become
Your manager.

COLUMBINE: Why, Pierrot, *I* can't act.

PIERROT: Can't act! Can't act! La, listen to
the woman!
What's that to do with the price of furs? —
You're blonde,
Are you not? — you have no education, have
you? —
Can't act! You underrate yourself, my dear!

COLUMBINE: Yes, I suppose I do.

PIERROT: As for the rest,
I'll teach you how to cry, and how to die,
And other little tricks; and the house will love
you.
You'll be a star by five o'clock . . . that is,
If you will let me pay for your apartment.

COLUMBINE: *Let* you? — well, that's a good one!
Ha! Ha! Ha!
But why?

PIERROT: But why? — well, as to that, my dear,
I cannot say.   It's just a matter of form.

COLUMBINE: Pierrot, I'm getting tired of caviar
And peacocks' livers.   Isn't there something else
That people eat? — some humble vegetable,
That grows in the ground?

PIERROT: Well, there are mushrooms.

COLUMBINE: Mushrooms!
That's so!   I had   forgotten . . . mushrooms
. . . mushrooms. . . .
I cannot *live* with . . . How do you like this
gown?

PIERROT: Not much.   I'm tired of gowns that have
the waist-line
About the waist, and the hem around the bottom,—
And women with their breasts in front of them!'—
Zut and ehè!   Where does one go from here!

COLUMBINE: Here's a persimmon, love. You always
liked them.

PIERROT: I am become a critic; there is nothing
I can enjoy. . . . However, set it aside;
I'll eat it between meals.

COLUMBINE: Pierrot, do you know,
Sometimes I think you're making fun of me.

PIERROT: My love, by yon black moon, you wrong
us both.

COLUMBINE: There isn't a sign of a moon, Pierrot.

PIERROT: Of course not.
There never was. "Moon's" just a word to swear
by.
"Mutton!" — now *there's* a thing you can lay the
hands on,
And set the tooth in! Listen, Columbine:
I always lied about the moon and you.
Food is my only lust.

COLUMBINE: Well, eat it, then,
For Heaven's sake, and stop your silly noise!
I haven't heard the clock tick for an hour.

PIERROT: It's ticking all the same. If you were a fly,

You would be dead by now. And if I were a
    parrot,
I could be talking for a thousand years!

(*Enter* COTHURNUS.)

PIERROT: Hello, what's this, for God's sake? —
What's the matter?
Say, whadda you mean? — get off the stage, my
    friend,
And pinch yourself, — you're walking in your sleep!

COTHURNUS: I never sleep.

PIERROT: Well, anyhow, clear out.
You don't belong on here. Wait for your own
    scene!
Whadda you think this is,— a dress-rehearsal?

COTHURNUS: Sir, I am tired of waiting. I will wait
No longer.

PIERROT: Well, but whadda you going to do?
The scene is set for me!

COTHURNUS: True, sir; yet I
Can play the scene.

PIERROT: Your scene is down for later!

COTHURNUS: That, too, is true, sir; but I play it now.

PIERROT: Oh, very well! — Anyway, I am tired
Of black and white. At least, I think I am.

(*Exit* COLUMBINE.)

Yes, I am sure I am. I know what I'll do! —
I'll go and strum the moon, that's what I'll do. . . .
Unless, perhaps . . . you never can tell . . . I may
be,
You know, tired of the moon. Well, anyway,
I'll go find Columbine. . . . And when I find her,
I will address her thus: "*Ehè,* Pierrette!" —
There's something in that.

(*Exit* PIERROT.)

COTHURNUS: You, Thyrsis! Corydon!
Where are you?

THYRSIS: (*Off stage.*) Sir, we are in our dressing-
room!

COTHURNUS: Come out and do the scene.

CORYDON: (*Off stage.*) You are mocking us! —
The scene is down for later.

COTHURNUS: That is true;
But we will play it now.   I am the scene.
(*Seats himself on high place in back of stage.*)

(*Enter* CORYDON *and* THYRSIS.)

CORYDON: Sir, we are counting on this little hour.
We said, "Here is an hour,— in which to think
A mighty thought, and sing a trifling song,
And look at nothing."— And, behold! the hour,
Even as we spoke, was over, and the act begun,
Under our feet!

THYRSIS: Sir, we are not in the fancy
To play the play.   We had thought to play it
later.

CORYDON: Besides, this is the setting for a farce.
Our scene requires a wall; we cannot build
A wall of tissue-paper!

THYRSIS: We cannot act
A tragedy with comic properties!

COTHURNUS: Try it and see.   I think you'll find
you can.
One wall is like another.   And regarding
The matter of your insufficient mood,

The important thing is that you speak the lines,
And make the gestures.   Wherefore I shall remain
Throughout, and hold the prompt-book.   Are you ready?

CORYDON-THYRSIS: (*Sorrowfully.*)   Sir, we are always ready.

COTHURNUS: Play the play!
(CORYDON *and* THYRSIS *move the table and chairs
    to one side out of the way, and seat them-
    selves in a half-reclining position on the
    floor.*)

THYRSIS: How gently in the silence, Corydon,
Our sheep go up the bank.   They crop a grass
That's yellow where the sun is out, and black
Where the clouds drag their shadows.   Have you noticed
How steadily, yet with what a slanting eye
They graze?

CORYDON: As if they thought of other things.
What say you, Thyrsis, do they only question

Where next to pull? — Or do their far minds
draw them
Thus vaguely north of west and south of east?

THYRSIS: One cannot say. . . . The black lamb
wears its burdocks
As if they were a garland,— have you noticed?
Purple and white — and drinks the bitten grass
As if it were a wine.

CORYDON: I've noticed that.
What say you, Thyrsis, shall we make a song
About a lamb that thought himself a shepherd?

THYRSIS: Why, yes! — that is, why,— no. (I have
forgotten my line.)

COTHURNUS: (*Prompting.*) "I know a game worth
two of that!"

THYRSIS: Oh, yes. . . . I know a game worth two
of that!
Let's gather rocks, and build a wall between us;
And say that over there belongs to me,
And over here to you!

CORYDON: Why,— very well.
And say you may not come upon my side
Unless I say you may!

THYRSIS: Nor you on mine!
And if you should, 'twould be the worse for you!
(*They weave a wall of colored crêpe paper ribbons
from the centre front to the centre back of the
stage, fastening the ends to* COLUMBINE'S *chair
in front and to* PIERROT'S *chair in the back.*)

CORYDON: Now there's a wall a man may see
across,
But not attempt to scale.

THYRSIS: An excellent wall.

CORYDON: Come, let us separate, and sit alone
A little while, and lay a plot whereby
We may outdo each other. (*They seat themselves
on opposite sides of the wall.*)

PIERROT: (*Off stage.*) Ehè, Pierrette!

COLUMBINE: (*Off stage.*) My name is Columbine!
Leave me alone!

THYRSIS: (*Coming up to the wall.*)
Corydon, after all, and in spite of the fact
I started it myself, I do not like this
So very much. What is the sense of saying
I do not want you on my side the wall?

It is a silly game. I'd much prefer
Making the little song you spoke of making,
About the lamb, you know, that thought himself
A shepherd! — what do you say?

(*Pause.*)

CORYDON: (*At wall.*) (I have forgotten the line.)

COTHURNUS: (*Prompting.*) "How do I know this
isn't a trick?"

CORYDON: Oh, yes. . . . How do I know this isn't
a trick
To get upon my land?

THYRSIS: Oh, Corydon,
You *know* it's not a trick. I do not like
The game, that's all. Come over here, or let
me
Come over there.

CORYDON: It is a clever trick
To get upon my land. (*Seats himself as before.*)

THYRSIS: Oh, very well! (*Seats himself as before.*)
(*To himself.*) I think I never knew a sillier game.

CORYDON: (*Coming to wall.*)
Oh, Thyrsis, just a minute! — all the water

Is on your side the wall, and the sheep are thirsty.
I hadn't thought of that.

THYRSIS: Oh, hadn't you?

CORYDON: Why, what do you mean?

THYRSIS: What do I mean? — I mean
That I can play a game as well as you can.
And if the pool is on my side, it's on
My side, that's all.

CORYDON: You mean you'd let the sheep
Go thirsty?

THYRSIS: Well, they're not my sheep. My sheep
Have water enough.

CORYDON: *Your* sheep! You are mad, to call them
Yours — mine — they are all one flock! Thyrsis,
    you can't mean
To keep the water from them, just because
They happened to be grazing over here
Instead of over there, when we set the wall up?

THYRSIS: Oh, can't I? — wait and see! — and if you
    try
To lead them over here, you'll wish you hadn't!

CORYDON: I wonder how it happens all the water
Is on your side. . . . I'll say you had an eye out
For lots of little things, my innocent friend,
When I said, "Let us make a song," and you said,
"I know a game worth two of that!"

COLUMBINE: (*Off stage.*)   Pierrot,
D'you know, I think you must be getting old,
Or fat, or something,— stupid, anyway! —
Can't you put on some other kind of collar?

THYRSIS: You know as well as I do, Corydon,
I never thought anything of the kind.
Don't you?

CORYDON: I *do* not.

THYRSIS: Don't you?

CORYDON: Oh, I suppose so.
Thyrsis, let's drop this,— what do you say? — it's
  only
A game, you know . . . we seem to be forgetting
It's only a game . . . a pretty serious game
It's getting to be, when one of us is willing
To let the sheep go thirsty for the sake of it.

THYRSIS: I know it, Corydon.
(*They reach out their arms to each other across the*
  wall.)

COTHURNUS: (*Prompting.*)   "But how do I
  know ——"

THYRSIS: Oh, yes. . . . But how do I know this isn't
  a trick
To water your sheep, and get the laugh on me?

CORYDON: You can't know, that's the difficult thing
  about it,
Of course,— you can't be sure. You have to take
My word for it. And I know just how you feel.
But one of us has to take a risk, or else,
Why, don't you see?— the game goes on for-
  ever! . . .
It's terrible, when you stop to think of it. . . .
Oh, Thyrsis, now for the first time I feel
This wall is actually a wall, a thing
Come up between us, shutting you away
From me. . . . I do not know you any more!

THYRSIS: No, don't say that! Oh, Corydon, I'm
  willing
To drop it all, if you will! Come on over

And water your sheep! It is an ugly game.
I hated it from the first. . . . How did it start?

CORYDON: I do not know . . . I do not know . . .
   I think
I am afraid of you! — you are a stranger!
I never set eyes on you before! "Come over
And water my sheep," indeed! — They'll be more
   thirsty
Than they are now before I bring them over
Into your land, and have you mixing them up
With yours, and calling them yours, and trying to
   keep them!

(Enter COLUMBINE*)*

COLUMBINE: (*To* COTHURNUS.) Glummy, I want
my hat.

THYRSIS: Take it, and go.

COLUMBINE: Take it and go, indeed. Is it my hat,
Or isn't it? Is this my scene, or not?
Take it and go! Really, you know, you two
Are awfully funny!

(Exit COLUMBINE*)*

THYRSIS: Corydon, my friend,
I'm going to leave you now, and whittle me

A pipe, or sing a song, or go to sleep.

When you have come to your senses, let me know.

(*Goes back to where he has been sitting, lies down
and sleeps.*)

(CORYDON, *in going back to where he has been sitting,
stumbles over bowl of colored confetti and colored
paper ribbons.*)

CORYDON: Why, what is this?— Red stones — and
purple stones —

And stones stuck full of gold! — The ground is
full

Of gold and colored stones! . . . I'm glad the wall

Was up before I found them! — Otherwise,

I should have had to share them. As it is,

They all belong to me. . . . Unless — (*He goes to
wall and digs up and down the length of it, to
see if there are jewels on the other side.*)   None
here ——

None here — none here — They all belong to me!
(*Sits.*)

THYRSIS: (*Awakening.*)   How curious!   I thought
the little black lamb

Came up and licked my hair; I saw the wool

About its neck as plain as anything!

It must have been a dream. The little black lamb
Is on the other side of the wall, I'm sure. (*Goes
to wall and looks over.* CORYDON *is seated on
the ground, tossing the confetti up into the air
and catching it.*)
Hello, what's that you've got there, Corydon?

CORYDON: Jewels.

THYRSIS: Jewels? — And where did you ever get
them?

CORYDON: Oh, over here.

THYRSIS: You mean to say you found them,
By digging around in the ground for them?

CORYDON: (*Unpleasantly.*)   No, Thyrsis,
By digging down for water for my sheep.

THYRSIS: Corydon, come to the wall a minute,
will you?
I want to talk to you.

CORYDON: I haven't time.
I'm making me a necklace of red stones.

THYRSIS: I'll give you all the water that you want,
For one of those red stones, — if it's a good one.

CORYDON: Water? — what for? — what do I want
of water?

THYRSIS: Why, for your sheep!

CORYDON: My sheep? — I'm not a shepherd!

THYRSIS: Your sheep are dying of thirst.

CORYDON: Man, haven't I told you
I can't be bothered with a few untidy
Brown sheep all full of burdocks? — I'm a mer-
chant.
That's what I am! — And if I set my mind to it
I dare say I could be an emperor!
(*To himself.*) Wouldn't I be a fool to spend my
time
Watching a flock of sheep go up a hill,
When I have these to play with? — when I have
these
To think about? — I can't make up my mind
Whether to buy a city, and have a thousand
Beautiful girls to bathe me, and be happy
Until I die, or build a bridge, and name it
The Bridge of Corydon, — and be remembered
After I'm dead.

THYRSIS: Corydon, come to the wall,
Won't you? — I want to tell you something.

CORYDON: Hush!
Be off! Be off! Go finish your nap, I tell you!

THYRSIS: Corydon, listen: if you don't want your
sheep,
Give them to me.

CORYDON: Be off! Go finish your nap.
A red one — and a blue one — and a red one —
And a purple one — give you my sheep, did you
say? —
Come, come! What do you take me for, a fool?
I've a lot of thinking to do,— and while I'm
thinking,
The sheep might just as well be over here
As over there. . . . A blue one — and a red one —

THYRSIS: But they will die!

CORYDON: And a green one — and a couple
Of white ones, for a change.

THYRSIS: Maybe I have
Some jewels on my side.

CORYDON: And another green one —
Maybe, but I don't think so.   You see, this rock
Isn't so very wide.   It stops before
It gets to the wall.   It seems to go quite deep,
However.

THYRSIS: (*With hatred.*)   I see.

COLUMBINE: (*Off stage.*)   Look, Pierrot, there's the
    moon.

PIERROT: (*Off stage.*)   Nonsense!

THYRSIS: I see.

COLUMBINE: (*Off stage.*)   Sing me an old song,
    Pierrot,—
Something I can remember.

PIERROT: (*Off stage.*)   Columbine.
Your mind is made of crumbs,— like an escallop
Of oysters,— first a layer of crumbs, and then
An oystery taste, and then a layer of crumbs.

THYRSIS: (*Searching.*)   I find no jewels . . . but I
    wonder what
The root of this black weed would do to a man
If he should taste it. . . . I have seen a sheep die,
With half the stalk still drooling from its mouth.

'Twould be a speedy remedy, I should think,
For a festered pride and a feverish ambition.
It has a curious root. I think I'll hack it
In little pieces. . . . First I'll get me a drink;
And then I'll hack that root in little pieces
As small as dust, and see what the color is
Inside. (*Goes to bowl on floor.*)

                     The pool is very clear. I see
A shepherd standing on the brink, with a red cloak
About him, and a black weed in his hand. . . .
'Tis I. (*Kneels and drinks.*)

CORYDON: (*Coming to wall.*) Hello, what are you
    doing, Thyrsis?

THYRSIS: Digging for gold.

CORYDON: I'll give you all the gold
You want, if you'll give me a bowl of water.
If you don't want too much, that is to say.

THYRSIS: Ho, so you've changed your mind? — It's
    different,
Isn't it, when you want a drink yourself?

CORYDON: Of course it is.

THYRSIS: Well, let me see . . . a bowl
Of water,— come back in an hour, Corydon.
I'm busy now.

CORYDON: Oh, Thyrsis, give me a bowl
Of water! — and I'll fill the bowl with jewels,
And bring it back!

THYRSIS: Be off, I'm busy now.
(*He catches sight of the weed, picks it up and looks
at it, unseen by* CORYDON.)
Wait! — Pick me out the finest stones you
have . . .
I'll bring you a drink of water presently.

CORYDON: (*Goes back and sits down, with the jewels
before him.*)
A bowl of jewels is a lot of jewels.

THYRSIS: (*Chopping up the weed.*) I wonder if it
has a bitter taste.

CORYDON: There's sure to be a stone or two among
them
I have grown fond of, pouring them from one hand
Into the other.

THYRSIS: I hope it doesn't taste
Too bitter, just at first.

CORYDON: A bowl of jewels
Is far too many jewels to give away
And not get back again.

THYRSIS: I don't believe
He'll notice. He's too thirsty. He'll gulp it down
And never notice.

CORYDON: There ought to be some way
To get them back again. . . . I could give him a
  necklace,
And snatch it back, after I'd drunk the water,
I suppose. . . . Why, as for that, of course a
  necklace. . . .

*(He puts two or three of the colored tapes together
and tries their strength by pulling them, after
which he puts them around his neck and pulls
them, gently, nodding to himself. He gets up
and goes to the wall, with the colored tapes in
his hands.)*

*(*THYRSIS *in the meantime has poured the powdered
root — black confetti — into the pot which con-
tained the flower and filled it up with wine from
the punch-bowl on the floor. He comes to the
wall at the same time, holding the bowl of
poison.)*

THYRSIS: Come, get your bowl of water, Corydon.

CORYDON: Ah, very good! — and for such a gift as that
I'll give you more than a bowl of unset stones.
I'll give you three long necklaces, my friend.
Come closer. Here they are. (*Puts the ribbons about* THYRSIS' *neck.*)

THYRSIS: (*Putting bowl to* CORYDON'S *mouth.*)
I'll hold the bowl
Until you've drunk it all.

CORYDON: Then hold it steady.
For every drop you spill I'll have a stone back
Out of this chain.

THYRSIS: I shall not spill a drop.
(CORYDON *drinks, meanwhile beginning to strangle* THYRSIS.)

THYRSIS: Don't pull the string so tight.

CORYDON: You're spilling the water.

THYRSIS: You've had enough — you've had enough — stop pulling
The string so tight!

CORYDON: Why, that's not tight at all . . .
How's this?

THYRSIS: (*Drops bowl.*)   You're strangling me!
Oh, Corydon!
It's only a game! — and you are strangling me!

CORYDON: It's only a game, is it? — Yet I believe
You've poisoned me in earnest! (*Writhes and
pulls the strings tighter, winding them about
THYRSIS' neck.*)

THYRSIS: Corydon! (*Dies.*)

CORYDON: You've poisoned me in earnest. . . . I
feel so cold. . . .
So cold . . . this is a very silly game. . . .
Why do we play it?— let's not play this game
A minute more . . . let's make a little song
About a lamb. . . . I'm coming over the wall,
No matter what you say,— I want to be near
you. . . .

(*Groping his way, with arms wide before him, he
strides through the frail papers of the wall without knowing it, and continues seeking for the
wall straight across the stage.*)

Where is the wall? (*Gropes his way back, and stands very near* THYRSIS *without seeing him; he speaks slowly.*)

There isn't any wall,
I think.   (*Takes a step forward, his foot touches* THYRSIS' *body, and he falls down beside him.*)

Thyrsis, where is your cloak? — just give me
A little bit of your cloak! . . . (*Draws corner of* THYRSIS' *cloak over his shoulders, falls across* THYRSIS' *body, and dies.*)

(COTHURNUS *closes the prompt-book with a bang, arises matter-of-factly, comes down stage, and places the table over the two bodies, drawing down the cover so that they are hidden from any actors on the stage, but visible to the audience, pushing in their feet and hands with his boot. He then turns his back to the audience, and claps his hands twice.*)

COTHURNUS: Strike the scene! (*Exit* COTHURNUS.)
          (*Enter* PIERROT *and* COLUMBINE.)

PIERROT: Don't puff so, Columbine!

COLUMBINE: Lord, what a mess
This set is in! If there's one thing I hate
Above everything else,— even more than getting
my feet wet —
It's clutter! — He might at least have left the
scene
The way he found it . . . don't you say so,
Pierrot?

(*She picks up punch bowl. They arrange chairs as
before at ends of table.*)

PIERROT: Well, I don't know. I think it rather
diverting
The way it is. (*Yawns, picks up confetti
bowl.*) Shall we begin?

COLUMBINE: (*Screams.*) My God!
What's that there under the table?

PIERROT: It is the bodies
Of the two shepherds from the other play.

COLUMBINE: (*Slowly.*) How curious to strangle
him like that,
With colored paper ribbons.

PIERROT: Yes, and yet
  I dare say he is just as dead. (*Pauses. Calls.*)
    Cothurnus!
  Come drag these bodies out of here! We can't
  Sit down and eat with two dead bodies lying
  Under the table! . . . The audience wouldn't
    stand for it!

COTHURNUS: (*Off stage.*) What makes you think
    so? —
  Pull down the tablecloth
  On the other side, and hide them from the house,
  And play the farce. The audience will forget.

PIERROT: That's so. Give me a hand there,
    Columbine.

(PIERROT *and* COLUMBINE *pull down the table cover
  in such a way that the two bodies are hidden
  from the house, then merrily set their bowls back
  on the table, draw up their chairs, and begin the
  play exactly as before.*)

COLUMBINE: Pierrot, a macaroon,— I cannot *live*
  without a macaroon!

PIERROT: My only love,
You are *so* intense! . . . Is it Tuesday, Colum-
    bine? —
I'll kiss you if it's Tuesday. (*Curtains begin to
    close slowly.*)

COLUMBINE: It is Wednesday,
If you must know. . . . Is this my artichoke
Or yours?

PIERROT: Ah, Columbine, as if it mattered!
Wednesday. . . . Will it be Tuesday, then, to-
    morrow,
By any chance? . . .

[CURTAIN.]

AUTHOR'S NOTE

ON THE PLAYING OF

ARIA DA CAPO

ORIGINAL CAST

[AS PLAYED BY THE PROVINCETOWN PLAYERS, NEW YORK CITY]

PIERROT	HARRISON DOWD
COLUMBINE	NORMA MILLAY
COTHURNUS	HUGH FERRISS
CORYDON	CHARLES ELLIS
THYRSIS	JAMES LIGHT

AUTHOR'S NOTE

SO great is my vexation always, when reading a play, to find its progress constantly being halted and its structure loosened by elaborate explanatory parentheses, that I resolved when I should publish *Aria da Capo* to incorporate into its text only those explanations the omission of which might confuse the reader or lend a wrong interpretation to the lines. Since, however, *Aria da Capo* was written not only to be read but also to be acted, and being conscious that the exclusion of the usual directions, while clarifying the play to the reader, may make it bare of suggestions and somewhat baffling to the producer, I am adding here some remarks which have been found of value in preparing it for presentation on the stage.

Since the production of *Aria da Capo* by the Provincetown Players, I have received a great many letters from the directors of little theatres, asking for copies of it with a view to producing it. Very often, after I send the play, I receive a letter in reply asking for some suggestions for its presentation, and enclosing direct questions on points that have been difficult. It occurred to me finally that it would be reasonable to make up a sort of informal prompt-book to send about with the play; and it is that which is printed below. It will be found incomplete and uneven, in some instances unnecessarily detailed, in others not sufficiently so; all of which is due to the fact that it was put together loosely, from answers to chance questions, rather than logically, as an entity in itself.

SUGGESTIONS FOR THE PRODUCTION OF "ARIA DA CAPO"

SETTING:

The setting required is simple: — a grey curtain, a long black table, two slender black high-backed chairs, and a raised platform.

Instead of wings and back-drop the Provincetown Players cleverly utilized painted screens, the heights varying from 6 to 10 feet, these being set right and left of the stage in such manner as to give the effect of depth and distance.

The table, six feet long and two feet wide, has thin legs and is painted black.

When Pierrot and Columbine enter in the final scene, it is not necessary that the table which Cothurnus has replaced shall entirely conceal the bodies of Thyrsis and Corydon. Pierrot and Columbine must ignore them until the lines indicate their discovery, no matter how they may have fallen.

Particular attention must be given to the chairs

39

in this set. They are used to construct the tissue-paper wall, and, although delicate, should be heavy enough to remain solid and steady, up and down stage, without the possibility of an upset when Corydon strides through the wall.

Near the footlights (actors' left) are two sofa pillows, used to represent the rocks against which the shepherds lean. On the left of the stage have another pillow, which Thyrsis places under his head when he lies down to sleep. Use cloth or crêpe paper for these pillows, and have them of spotted black and white material, or of any gay color except red or blue.

Cothurnus occupies a chair upon a platform, up-stage, centre, with two or three steps surrounding it on three sides. Drape this with plain heavy black cloth.

The table covering is important. Its width is equal to that of the added height and width of the table. As it must be moved to cover the bodies of Thyrsis and Corydon, it should be of sufficient weight to prevent slipping. It will be well to experiment with this, to ensure proper performance.

The cover should have black and white spots and striped ends.

The table is set as follows: — two large wooden
bowls (at least seven inches high and fourteen inches
in diameter). One is placed at each end of the table.
That at Columbine's end should contain persimmons,
pomegranates, grapes and other bright exotic fruits.
Pierrot's bowl has confetti and colored paper ribbons,
the latter showing plainly over the edge. (If Columbine uses practical macaroons, put them into this
bowl.)

Near Columbine, place a practical uncooked
artichoke; have this of good size, and nail it to a
wooden standard, painted black. At both places there
are tall white wooden goblets.

In the centre of the table there should be a curious,
grotesque, but very gay flower, standing upright in a
pot of wood or heavy paper, which will not break
when Thyrsis drops it. Concealed at the root of this
plant there should be a small sack of black confetti,
to be used in the "poison scene."

The table should be set with nothing but these
articles, and yet give the appearance of bounty and
elegance.

Place the table parallel with the footlights,— the
long side toward the audience.

Columbine's chair is at the actors' right, and Pierrot's opposite — Columbine's hat hangs from her chair-top. Both chairs are festooned with tissue-paper ribbons, at least ten feet long, to be used later by the shepherds to represent their wall. These must be of such a texture as to break readily when Corydon walks through, and a prearranged transverse tear or two will assist in the prompt breakage when he does so.

PROPERTIES:

Two white wooden bowls, one filled with fruits and the other with confetti and paper ribbons,— one ribbon to be of cotton or silk, in order to be not too easily broken by Corydon when strangling Thyrsis

Two tall white wooden goblets

One artichoke nailed to a standard

One flower in paper or wooden pot, the root wrapped with black crêpe paper (or use confetti)

Black and white tablecloth

Macaroons

Boots and prompt-book for Cothurnus (large flat black book)

Also, if desired, mask of Tragedy for Cothurnus

Crêpe or tissue streamers of different colors, including no red or blue, for wall.

Costumes:

PIERROT: Lavender or lilac satin, preferably a blue-lavender. Care should be taken that the lavender does not turn pink under the stage lights. Pierrot's costume is the conventional smock with wide trousers, with black crêpe paper rosettes on the smock, wide white tarleton ruff. Black evening pumps with black rosettes may be worn. Black silk skull-cap.

COLUMBINE: Tight black satin bodice cut very low, with straps over the shoulders, quite like the modern evening gown; very full tarleton skirts of different shades of pink and cerise, reaching to the knees; ruffled bloomers of apple-green tarleton, the ruffles showing below the skirts; black silk stockings and black ballet slippers, laced with green. Hat of lavender crêpe paper, with streamers of gay colors — including, however, no clear red or blue. Hat should be small and very smart — not a *shepherdess* hat. Columbine should be made up to suggest a doll. As originally interpreted she had short light hair, standing out bushily all over her head. Long hair should be rolled under to give a *bobbed* effect, or could be arranged in obvious caricature of some extreme modern style, but must look attractive, and must be blonde.

COTHURNUS: Plain toga of dull purple in some heavy, unreflecting material which will fall into large folds, lined with sombre flame-color; a garment with large purple sleeves, of which only the sleeves were visible, was worn under the toga,— but the effect should be classical; heavy boots should be worn, as nearly as possible like the tragic Roman buskin; one end of the great toga is tied into a rough hood which covers the actor's head; a mask may be worn, but it is often difficult to speak through, and, if desired, the actor's face may be made up to represent a mask of Tragedy.

THYRSIS and CORYDON: These costumes, in striking contrast to the elegance of those of Pierrot and Columbine, should be very simple, and very roughly made; short tunics of outing-flannel or some such material — fastened loosely over one shoulder,— one shoulder, as well as most of the back and breast, exposed. Legs bare, or swathed from the knee to the ankle in rough strips of the same material. Sandals. Cloaks of heavier, cheap material fastened to the tunics in such a way that they will appear to be simply flung over the shoulder, but actually fastened very cleverly in order to avoid tripping the shepherds, who are continually sitting down on the floor and getting up again.

Thyrsis wears a dark grey tunic and cloak of raw bright red,— but not a turkey-red, as this color will kill the blue of Corydon's cloak. Corydon wears tunic of light grey and cloak of brilliant blue. There must be no red or blue used anywhere in the entire play excepting in the blue and red of these two cloaks. The two shepherds must be so strong and vivid in every way that when Columbine comes in and says, "Is this my scene or not?" it will seem to the audience that it is she, not the shepherds, who is hopelessly out of the scene.

CHARACTERS:

PIERROT: Pierrot sees clearly into existing evils and is rendered gaily cynical by them; he is both too indolent and too indifferent to do anything about it. Yet in several lines of the play his actual unhappiness is seen, — for instance, "Moon's just a word to swear by," in which he expresses his conviction that all beauty and romance are fled from the world. At the end of the play the line, "Yes, and yet I dare say he is just as dead," must not be said flippantly or cynically, but slowly and with much philosophic concentration on the thought. From the moment when Columbine cries, "What's that there under the table?" until Pierrot calls, "Cothurnus, come drag these bodies out of here!" they both stand staring at the two bodies, without moving in any way, or even lifting their eyes. (This same *holding* of the play is used several times also by the shepherds,— for instance, always during the off-stage interpolations, they stand either staring at each other across the wall, or maintaining whatever other position they may have had when the off-stage voice begins speaking, until the interruption is over, when they resume their drama quite as if nobody had spoken.) Columbine's "How curious to strangle him like that" is spoken extremely slowly, in a voice of awe, curiosity, and horror. For a moment the two characters seem almost to feel and be subdued by the tragedy that has taken place. They remain standing very quietly while Cothurnus speaks his final lines off stage, and for a moment after he has said, "The audience will forget"; then very slowly raise their eyes and exchange glances, Pierrot nods his head curtly and says, "That's so"; they set their bowls gaily back on the table, and the play begins again.

Pierrot in such lines as "Ah, Columbine, as if it
mattered!" speaks with mock saccharine tenderness;
but in such lines as "If you were a fly you would be
dead by now!" although he speaks very gaily his malice
must be apparent almost even to her; Columbine bores
him to death. When he says, "I'll go and strum the
moon!" he is for the instant genuinely excited and
interested; he is for this moment like a child, and is
happy.

COLUMBINE: Pretty and charming, but stupid; she
never knows what Pierrot is talking about, and is so
accustomed to him that she no longer pretends to
understand him; but she is very proud of him, and
when he speaks she listens with trustful admiration.
Her expression, "I cannot live without" this or that,
is a phrase she uses in order to make herself more
attractive, because she believes men prefer women to
be useless and extravagant; if left to herself she would
be a domestic and capable person.

COTHURNUS: This character should be played by a
tall and imposing figure with a tremendous voice.
The voice of Cothurnus is one of the most important
things in the acting play. He should have a voice

deeper than the voice used by any of the other persons, should speak weightily and with great dignity, but almost without intonation, and quite without feeling, as if he had said the same words many times before. Only in his last speech may he be permitted a comment on the situation. This speech should be spoken quite as impressively as the others and fully as slowly.

CORYDON and THYRSIS: These two characters are young, very simple, and childlike; they are acted upon by the force that sits on the back of the stage behind them. More and more as their quarrel advances they begin to see that something is wrong, but they have no idea what to do about it, and they scarcely realize what is happening, the quarrel grows so from little things into big things. Corydon's first vision of the tragedy is in "It's terrible when you stop to think of it." Thyrsis' first vision comes when he looks into the pool; in seeing the familiar reflection he is struck by the unfamiliarity of one aspect of it, the poisonous root; for the first time he realizes that this man who is about to kill with poisoned water his most beloved friend, is none other than Thyrsis *himself*,—" 'Tis I!" The personalities of Thyrsis and Corydon are not

essentially different. They develop somewhat differ-
ently, because of the differing circumstances.

When Columbine goes out for the first time she
takes with her her artichoke and her wine-glass, also
a couple of macaroons, which she nibbles, going out.
This helps to get the table cleared. The other articles
are removed by the shepherds when they prepare the
stage for their scene, in this manner: at the cue "Sir,
we are always ready. . . . Play the play!", Corydon
and Thyrsis come down stage, Corydon to Pierrot's
end of the table, Thyrsis to Columbine's; simul-
taneously, first, they set back the chairs against the
wall, Pierrot's left front, Columbine's right front;
next they remove the two big bowls and set them in
symmetrical positions on the floor, left front and
right front, in such a way that the bowl of confetti
may be the mine of jewels for Corydon, and the bowl
of fruits, the punch-bowl, may represent the pool of
water for Thyrsis; then, taking the table by the two
ends, they set it back against the wall, right; next,
while Corydon places the two pillows from the left
wall on the floor to represent rocks in their pasture,
Thyrsis removes from the table everything that is left

on it except the tablecloth,—this should be only
Pierrot's wine-goblet and the flower in its pot. (The
flower is to represent later the poisonous weed which
Thyrsis finds, the wine-goblet a drinking-cup beside
the pool, the flower-pot a bowl in which to mix the
poison and bring it to Corydon.) The two shepherds
do this setting of their stage swiftly and silently, then
seat themselves at once, in easy but beautiful postures,
and remain for a moment looking off as if at their
sheep while a complete silence settles over the stage
and house,— a *pastoral* silence, if it is possible to suggest it — before they begin to speak.

When Columbine comes in, looking for her hat, she
picks up the hat from her chair, now in the centre of
the stage near the footlights, in a direct line with
Pierrot's, which is centre back, just in front of
Cothurnus,— the shepherds having set them in these
positions, back to back, in order to have their aid in
weaving the wall. After taking her hat, Columbine
stands looking at the shepherds to see what is going on.
They do not look at her. After a moment Thyrsis,
slowly, with his eyes steadfastly on Corydon's, says,
"Take it, and go." When Columbine comes in in the

final scene, she is wearing the hat. She takes it off, however, as she sits down again at the table, so that the second beginning of the play may recall as vividly as possible to the audience the first beginning.

Date Loaned

Date	Name
NOV 2 9 1932	E. Kless
	E. Fields
APR 6 1933	J. McDonald
APR 2 1 1933	Mrs Guyton
JAN 8 1937	" "
APR 14 1939	Miss Gerry
JUN 2 4 1939	C. Coolidge
MAY 1 1 1940	E. Majors
FEB 2 4 1952	Mr. Vinson
MAR 1 1 1952	Mr. Vinson
FEB 9 1959	Miss Sess H.
	M B Mullikin
AUG 1 1 1960	My Vinson
NOV 4 1961	John Jones
SEP 3 0 1993	